Algerian Plaited Stitch

This rich-looking textured stitch has been used on the pyramid-shaped structure in the foreground of the detail, 'Red Ship', opposite. Gobelin Straight Stitch, Gobelin Filling, Satin Stitch, Cross Stitch and Double Cross Stitch provide contrasting textures throughout the design and help to give the effect of distance behind the pyramid.

Tapisserie wool is used to work this design as follows: colour numbers 8212, 8456, 8524, 8672, 8818, 8914, 8920, 8924, 8004, 8530 and 8420.

Fig 1 *Bring the thread through at A and insert the needle at B 4 threads down and 2 threads to the right. Bring the needle through again at C, 2 threads to the left and level with B.*

Fig 2 *From C, insert the needle at D, 4 threads up and 4 to the right. Bring the needle through again at E, 2 threads to the left and level with D.*

Fig 3 *From E, insert the needle at F 4 threads down and 2 threads to the right, bringing the needle through again at B.*

Fig 4 *This shows the effect of 2 rows of Algerian Plaited Stitch.*

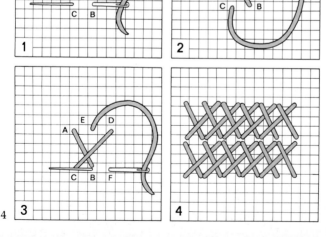

Red Ship ▶
A working chart for this design is on page 98

4

THE ANCHOR BOOK OF

Canvaswork
EMBROIDERY STITCHES

Compiled by Eve Harlow · DAVID & CHARLES

Contents

Introduction

This handy book of canvaswork stitches provides a superb reference source for anyone who is interested in this rewarding form of embroidery. It will be of particular interest to beginners, who are sure to find the variety of different textures that can be achieved with simple stitches fascinating.

All the most popular canvaswork stitches are demonstrated in clear step-by-step diagrams, and presented in alphabetical order to make quick reference simple. You will also find less well-known stitches collected here. Photographs show the finished effects which can be achieved and working charts for many of the designs are given towards the end of the book. The cover design is charted on page 103.

1

Algerian Filling

This stitch consists of groups of three straight stitches worked over 4 threads of canvas. In the 'Villas' design opposite Algerian stitch is worked vertically on the centre house's roof and horizontally on the pink house and green house walls.

This useful filling stitch is quick and easy to work and can add texture to pictorial designs.

Long Satin Stitch, Brick Stitch, Petit Point and Cross Stitches are also used in 'Villas', with a single French Knot used to indicate door knobs.

Fig 1 Bring the thread through at A and insert the needle at B, 4 threads above. Bring the needle through at C, 4 threads down and 1 thread to the left. Insert the needle at D 4 threads above and bring it out at E, 4 threads down and 1 thread to the left. Work E-F. Begin the next group of 3 stitches 4 threads to the left. Work A-B, C-D, E-F, then start the third group of stitches 4 threads to the left.

Fig 2 For the second row and working left to right, having worked the last stitch of the group of three, bring the needle out 3 threads to the right and 6 threads down at A. Insert the needle at B, 4 threads above and work C-D, E-F to continue the group of 3 stitches.

Fig 3 Continue working groups of 3 stitches in the spaces of the previous row. Work subsequent rows in the same way. To finish the edge, fill the top row with stitches worked over 2 threads of canvas.

Villas ▶

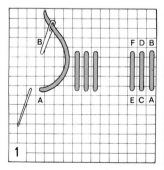

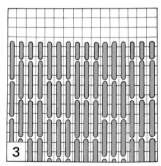

2

Brick Stitch

Brick Stitch and Gobelin Filling Stitch produce a very similar pattern. In Brick Stitch, each stitch is only two canvas threads long (Gobelin Filling Stitch is six threads long). The method for Brick Stitch produces single rows of stitches, each row forming a zigzag pattern across the canvas.

Fig 1 *Starting at right, work A-B over 2 threads of canvas, bringing the needle through at C.*

Fig 2 *From C, insert the needle at D, 2 threads of canvas above and bring the needle out at E, level with A.*

Fig 3 *Continue working stitches in the same way across the row. At the end of the row, reverse the working direction, positioning the bases of the new stitches 1 stitch length below the bases of the preceding row.*

Butterfly ▶

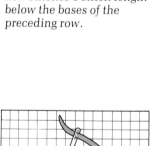

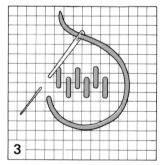

Broad Cross Stitch

The stitch has been used in the Diamonds design opposite to cover most of the canvas, with diamond shapes worked in Long Stitch for contrast.

The stitch occupies a square of 6 threads of canvas. Three vertical stitches are worked first, then 3 horizontal stitches are worked across them.

Fig 1 Bring the thread through at A, insert the needle at B, bring the thread out at C. Insert the needle at D and bring the thread out at E. Insert the needle at F and bring it out at G, 2 to the left and 2 below A, ready to begin the horizontal stitches.

Fig 2 Bring the thread through at G and insert the needle at H, 6 threads to the right and level with G.

Bring the needle through at I, 1 thread below G. Complete the Cross by working the third horizontal stitch.

Fig 3 Here, the second row of Broad Crosses is being worked. Having completed two Broad Crosses, insert the needle at L and bring it out ready to work the centre stitch of the 3 vertical stitches of the next Broad Cross (6 threads down, 6 to the left of L).

Work the left hand vertical stitch and then the right hand stitch to complete stage 1.

Then bring the needle out at S and insert the needle at T. Bring the thread through at U and insert the needle at V.

To complete the Broad Cross stitch, bring the needle through at W and then insert it at X, 1 thread below V.

Diamonds ▶

A working chart for this design is on page 98

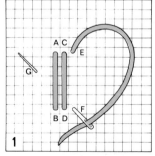

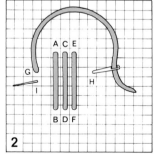

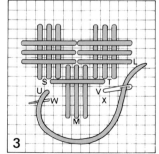

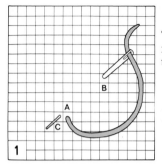

Byzantine Stitch

This stitch is worked diagonally across 4 (or more) vertical and horizontal threads.

Fig 1 Bring the thread through at A, and insert the needle at B 4 threads up and 4 threads to the right, bringing the needle through again at C, 1 thread to the left of A.

Fig 2 Continue working C-D, E-F, G-H, I-J, K-L, then, bringing the thread through at M 1 thread up from K, insert the needle at N, 1 thread up from L.

Fig 3 Continue, working the second 'step' in the same way.

Fig 4 Shows the second row of 'steps' fitting into the first row.

Blue Mood ▶

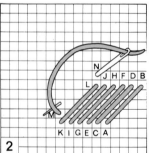

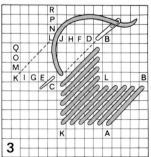

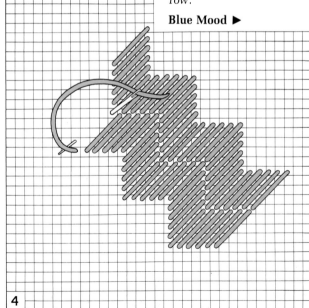

Chain Stitch

Worked in close rows, Chain Stitch produces an even texture that contrasts well with other stitches. In 'Seedhead', the design opposite, Chain Stitch is used for two large, central areas, with bands of Gobelin Filling and Satin Stitches. French Knots are used for the green tip of the seedhead.

Tapisserie wools in a toning range of colours are used in the design as follows: colour numbers 9314, 8508, 9324, 9636, 9306, 9536, 8264, 9310, 9554 and 9666.

Fig 1 Bring the thread through at A, hold the thread down with the thumb and insert the needle through the same hole at A. Bring the needle through 2 threads below at B keeping the thread under the needle.

Fig 2 Holding the thread down with the thumb, insert the needle in the same hole at B, keeping the thread under the needle. Bring the needle through at C 2 threads below B and pull through, keeping the thread under the needle.

Fig 3 Continue working close rows of Chain Stitches. Finish the last loop in each row with a small tying stitch, finishing the yarn end on the wrong side by interweaving through the backs of stitches.

Seedhead ▶

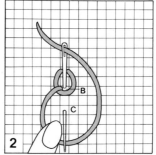

1

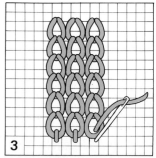

3

Chequer Stitch

This stitch pattern is formed by alternating Cushion Stitch with squares of Tent Stitch. Chequer Stitch is used for the background texture of the one-colour tile design 'Chequer Board' on the opposite page. Four other stitches have been included to produce the almost three-dimensional effect of this design — Satin Stitch, Cross Stitch, Gobelin Filling and Rhodes Stitch, set at the centre and in groups of three at the sides.

Tapisserie wool, colour 8804 is used to work this embroidery.

Fig 1 Cushion Stitch: Bring the thread through at A and work a diagonal stitch across 2 threads, inserting the needle at B, 1 thread up and 1 thread to the right. Bring the needle through at C, 1 thread below A and insert the needle at D 1 thread to the right of B. Continue as shown, working E-F, G-H, I-J, K-L, M-N.

Fig 2 From N, bring the needle through 2 threads down and immediately below N, inserting the needle again 1 thread up and 1 to the right to make the first stitch of the second Cushion. Continue, working E-F, G-H, I-J, K-L, M-N.

Fig 3 Work Tent Stitches over 1 vertical and 1 horizontal thread of canvas.

Fig 4 The finished effect of Cushion Stitch and Tent Stitch making Chequer Stitch.

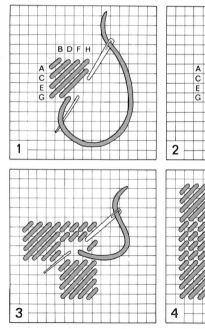

14

Chequer Board ▶

Cross Stitch

This is one of the basic canvas embroidery stitches and is formed as a cross by taking the thread diagonally over 2 horizontal and 2 vertical threads of canvas. Each cross is completed before passing on to the next. In all Cross Stitches and variations; the uppermost stitches should pass in the same direction.

The brilliantly coloured design 'Geraniums' on the opposite page could be used for a book or wallet cover or, if the design were completed at the edges, might form an attractive central panel for a decorative cushion.

French Knots are used for the flower centres, producing a three-dimensional effect and tiny Petit Point Stitches 'distance' the green background. Tapisserie wool is used in the design as follows: colour numbers 8212, 8204, 8392, 8436, 8456, 8416, 8542, 8524 and 9308.

Fig 1 *Bring the thread through at A and insert the needle at B, 2 threads up and 2 threads to the left. Bring the needle through at C, 2 threads below B.*

Fig 2 *From C, insert the needle at D, 2 threads up and 2 threads to the right. Bring the needle through at C again to complete the cross.*

Fig 3 *To work the second cross, insert the needle at E, 2 threads up and 2 threads to the left. Bring the needle through at F, 2 threads below E. Complete the cross as shown in Fig 2.*

Fig 4 *This shows 3 rows of Cross stitch.*

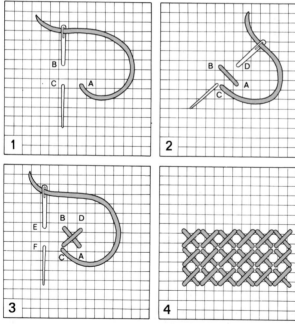

Geraniums ▶

Alternating Cross Stitch

This effective stitch pattern has been used for the road in the 'Little Town' design on the opposite page. Two tones of grey have been used, producing a decorative pattern that contrasts well with the less textured stitches used for the houses. Long Satin Stitch and Gobelin Filling are used for the walls and roofs with green Cross Stitches for the grass and foliage. Small areas of Petit Point stitch detail the windows, doors and tree trunks.

Fig 1 Bring the thread through at A and insert the needle at B, 6 threads up and 2 threads to the left. Bring the needle through at C, 6 threads down and 2 threads to the left of A, and insert the needle at D, 6 threads above A. Bring the needle through again at E, 2 threads above C.

Fig 2 To work the small Cross stitch, insert the needle at F, 2 threads up and 2 threads to the left. Bring the needle through at G, 2 threads below F.

Fig 3 Complete the small Cross as shown here, G-H.

Fig 4 This shows the finished stitch pattern of long Cross stitches and regular Cross stitches.

Little Town▶

Double Cross Stitch

This is a variation on the Cross stitch and has a Straight Cross Stitch on top. It makes a very decorative pattern in geometric designs such as the corner motif 'Squares and Zigzags' on the opposite page, where it has been used with Satin Stitch and chunky Rhodes stitches. Tapisserie wool is used to work the design.

Fig 1 Bring the thread through at A and insert the needle at B, 4 threads up and 4 to the left. Bring the needle through again at C, 4 threads below B and insert it at D, 4 threads above A, bringing it out again at E, 2 threads to the left and midway between C and A.

Fig 2 From E, insert the needle at F, 4 threads above and midway between B and D, bringing it out again at G, 2 threads below B and midway between B and C.

Fig 3 Complete the cross by taking the thread across from G and inserting the needle at H.

Fig 4 Double Crosses can be worked in horizontal or vertical rows, as in 'Squares and Zigzags' or can follow a design line.

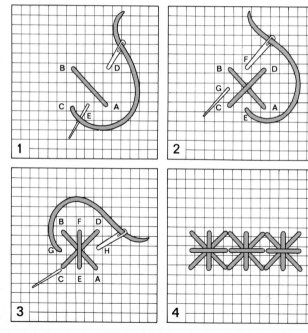

Squares and Zigzags ▶
A working chart for this design is on page 100

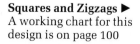

Double Straight Cross Stitch

This stitch is somewhat similar to Double Cross Stitch but is worked in a diamond shape, rather than a square. The first stage is a Straight Cross worked over 4 vertical and 4 horizontal threads. A diagonal Cross Stitch is superimposed worked over 2 vertical and 2 horizontal canvas thread intersections.

In the formalised design 'Pansy' on the opposite page, Double Straight Cross Stitch is used for the inner area of the petals, contrasting very effectively with the areas of Satin Stitches, Gobelin Filling Stitches and the Cross Cornered Cushion Stitches.

Fig 1 *Bring the thread through at A and insert the needle at B, 4 threads above. Bring the needle through at C, midway between A and B and 2 threads to the left. Insert the needle at D and bring it through at E, 1 thread down and 1 thread to the left.*

Fig 2 *From E, insert the needle at F, diagonally across and 2 threads up and 2 threads to the left. Bring the needle through at G, 2 threads below F.*

Fig 3 *From G, insert the needle at H diagonally across and 2 threads up and 2 threads to the right. Bring the needle through 3 threads down and 3 threads to the right, ready to begin the next Double Straight Cross Stitch.*

Fig 4 *shows 7 Double Straight Cross Stitches.*

Pansy ▶
A working chart for this design is on page 101

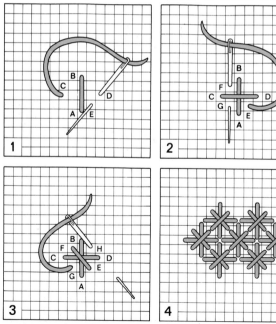

22

Double Plaited Cross Stitch

This is a more complex variation on Cross Stitch but it has an interesting texture and adds richness to designs as in 'Knot Garden' on the opposite page. Satin Stitch is the only other stitch used and illustrates the versatility of basic stitches when they are worked in different directions and over varying numbers of threads.

Fig 1 Work stitches 1-2, 3-4, bringing the needle out 1 thread to the right of the place you began.

Fig 2 Work stitch 5-6, bringing the needle out one stitch below 3 at 7.

Fig 3 Work stitch 7-8, then take the needle 4 threads up and 6 threads to the left and bring it through at 9. Insert the needle 6 threads down and 6 to the right at 10. Bring the needle through at 11, 6 threads up and 1 thread to the left.

Fig 4 Continue, following the sequence, remembering that the needle comes through on odd numbers and is inserted on even numbers.

Fig 5 This shows the finished stitch, with the last stitch worked being 15-16 which is slipped under instead of over stitch (9-10).

Knot Garden ▶

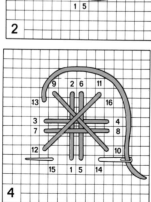

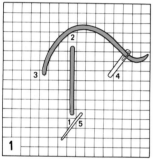

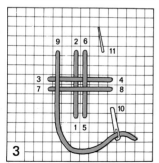

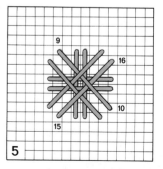

Half Cross Stitch

This is one of the most popular stitches in canvas embroidery. It resembles Petit Point Stitch in appearance but the working method is different. Half Cross Stitch consists of small diagonal stitches worked over 1 canvas thread intersection, with the stitches on the reverse side vertical.

Fig 1 Bring the thread through at A and insert the needle diagonally across over 1 canvas thread intersection at B. Bring the needle through at C, 1 thread below.

Fig 2 Work stitches C-D, E-F in the same way, bringing the needle through at G, ready to work the next stitch.

Fig 3 On the second row, the needle is passed vertically upwards to work the stitches. Having worked the last stitch O-P, bring the thread through at Q and insert the needle diagonally down over 1 canvas thread intersection at R. Bring the needle through 1 thread above.

Fig 4 Each row is worked in the same way, first left to right with the needle passed vertically downwards, then right to left with the needle passed vertically upwards.

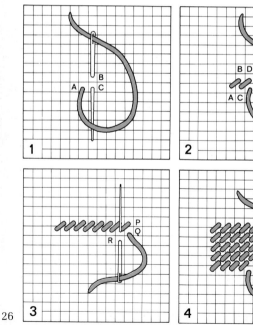

Daisies ▶

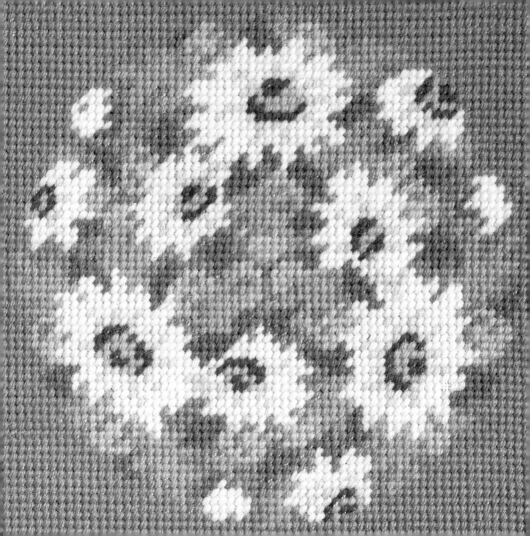

Long Armed Cross Stitch

This is known as Slav Cross Stitch and is worked from left to right in horizontal rows. In the 'Chess Board' design on the opposite page, Long-armed Cross Stitch is used in bands, shading from cream through pink and peach then tan to russet. This use of colour and stitch gives an exciting three-dimensional effect to the design.

Fig 1 Bring the thread through at A and insert the needle at B, 6 threads to the right and 3 threads up. Bring the needle through at C, immediately below B and level with A.

Fig 2 From C, insert the needle at D, 3 threads to the left and 3 threads up. Bring the needle through again at E, 3 canvas threads below D.

Fig 3 To begin the next Long-armed Cross, insert the needle at F, 3 threads to the right of B and bring it through at G, 3 canvas threads down.

Fig 4 shows 3 Long-armed Cross stitches worked and the needle has been inserted at J, to be brought through 3 threads below A at K, ready to work the second row.

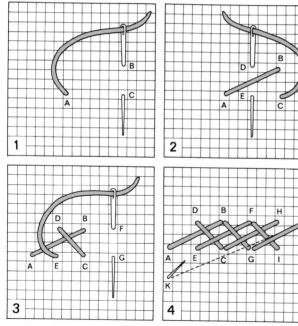

28

Chess Board▶

Oblong Cross Stitch

This stitch can be worked from right to left or left to right for the first half of the cross and is then completed on the return journey. It is important that the upper half of the cross lies in the same direction throughout.

The Corner Motif design on the opposite page is one quarter of a cushion cover and besides Oblong Cross Stitches, Gobelin Filling, Long Satin Stitches and Cross Stitches are used.

The design is worked in Tapisserie wools, colours as follows: 8734, 8706, 8302, 8306 and 9488.

Fig 1 *Bring the thread through on the lower right hand side at A, insert the needle 4 threads up and 2 threads to the left at B and bring it out 4 threads down at C, thus forming a half Oblong Cross Stitch. Continue to the end of the row, C-D, E-F, G-H.*

Fig 2 *To complete the stitch, bring the needle through at I and insert again at F, bringing it through at G.*

Fig 3 *This shows the second row of Oblong Cross stitches being worked.*

Corner Motif ▶

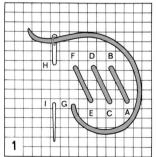

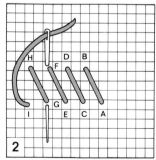

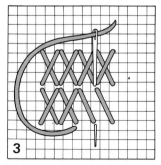

30

Upright Cross Stitch

This simple stitch has a variety of uses in providing areas of texture, especially when several stitches are being used together in one piece, such as the 'Village' detail on the opposite page. In this design, the stitch has been used on several of the roofs, contrasting well with the Long Satin Stitch and Parisian Stitch used on some of the walls.

The stitch is worked diagonally from lower right to upper left.

Fig 1 *Bring the thread through at A and insert the needle at B, 4 threads above. Bring the needle through at C, 2 threads down and 2 to the left, and insert it at D, 4 threads above. Continue in this way to the end of the row (G-H), bringing the needle through at I, ready to complete the stitch on the return journey.*

Fig 2 *From I, insert the needle at F, 4 threads to the right, and bring it out at G. To continue the sequence, insert the needle at D and bring it out at E, then work B-C.*

Fig 3 *From C, insert the needle at J, 4 threads to the right, then, to start the next row of Upright Cross Stitches, bring the needle through at K, 6 threads below and 2 threads to the left.*

Fig 4 *From K, insert the needle at A, 4 threads above, and bring it out at L, 2 threads down and 2 to the left. Continue the second row as Fig 1, then work Fig 2 and Fig 3.*

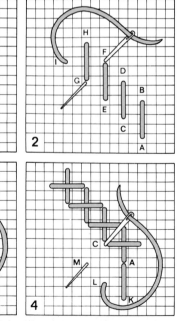

Village ▶

Cross-cornered Cushion Stitch

Figs 1 and 2 Starting at A-B, top left, work the square over 6 vertical and 6 horizontal threads. Work U-V then pass the needle under to emerge at the opposite corner (W).

Fig 3 From W, insert the needle at X (bottom right) and bring it through at Y, 1 thread to the right of W.

Fig 4 This shows the top right corner overworked. The last stitch at top right passes the needle 6 threads to the left and 2 threads up ready to begin the next cushion.

Fig 5 This shows the first stage of the cushion (as Fig 2) with the needle passing underneath ready to begin the overworking diagonal stitches at bottom right.

Fig 6 Four Cross-cornered Cushion Stitches with the overworked corners lying to the centre.

Squares ▶

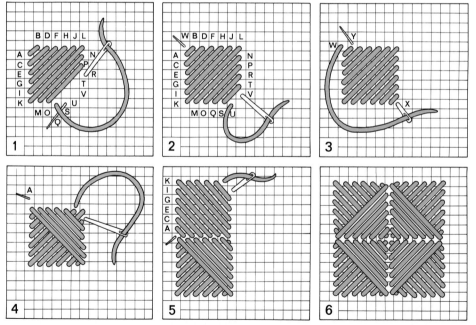

34

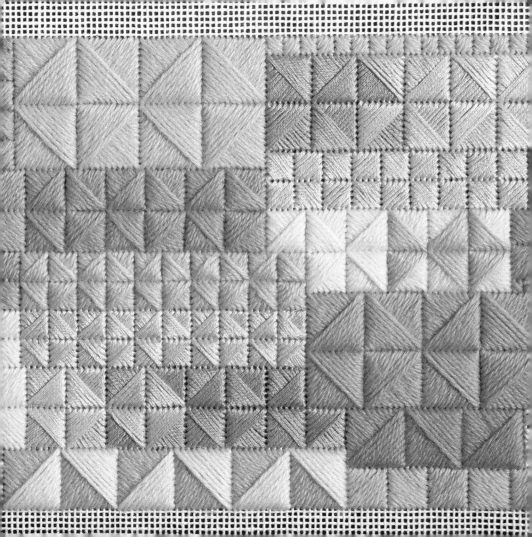

Diagonal Stitch

This stitch gives the effect of woven fabric or brocade when worked over a large surface area.

Fig 1 Bring the thread through at A and work a Straight Stitch diagonally over 2 canvas thread

intersections to B. Bring the needle out at C, 1 thread below A.

Fig 2 Work stitch C-D over 3 intersections, then E-F over 4 intersections. G-H is worked over 3 intersections, then I-J over 2 intersections.

Fig 3 Continue in the same

way K-L (over 3 intersections) M-N (over 4 intersections), O-P (over 3 intersections).

Fig 4 This shows the position of the following rows in relation to the first, where the longest stitches of one row fall diagonally below the shortest stitches of the previous row.

Ideas for the design

The pattern forms a close fabric and is thus ideal for chair seats and stool tops where there is likely to be considerable wear. It would also look extremely attractive used on fasion accessories, such as a matching bag and belt.

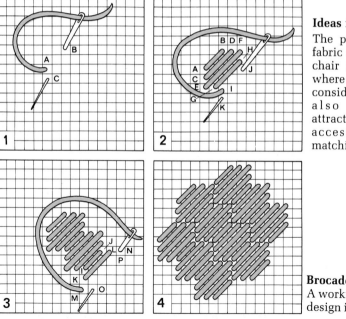

Brocade ▶
A working chart for this design is on page 102

36

Diamond Eyelet

In this stitch, individual stitches are worked from every hole around the perimeter into the centre hole.

Diamond Eyelet can be worked as a square or as a diamond shape, as in the design opposite. Here, Back Stitches outline each Di-amond shape, producing an effect which could be used for a cushion cover, a chair seat or a box top.

Worked on a finer mesh canvas and using Stranded Cotton, the design could also be worked for a belt or a bag.

Tapisserie wool is used to work the design as fol-lows: colour numbers 8914, 8806, 8804, 9192 and 9164.

Fig 1 *Bring the thread through at A and insert the needle at B, 5 threads below A. Bring the thread through at C, 1 intersection of canvas threads down to the right from A. Insert the needle at B again, bringing the needle out at D, 1 intersection down to the right from C.*

Fig 2 *Continue working stitches from the centre hole, B-E, B-F, B-G, B-H, B-I.*

Fig 3 *Continue the Eyelet as shown.*

Fig 4 *Work Back Stitches around each Eyelet.*

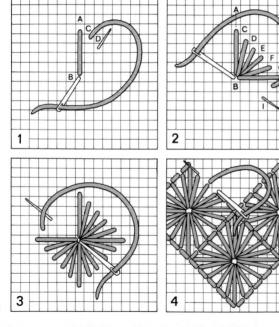

Diamond Eyelet ▶

Eyelet Hole

Here the Eyelet is worked in a square and to a finer scale, using Stranded Cotton. Combined with rectangles in Satin Stitch and Petit Point, an interesting textured fabric is achieved which could be used for the border of a cushion or for a curtain tieback. The design, 'Mosaic', might also be worked for a mirror frame or as an inset on a book cover.

The following colours are used to work the design: 075, 097, 0871, 0873, 0887, 0933 and 0970.

Fig 1 Bring the thread through at A and insert the needle at B, over 3 intersections of canvas threads. Bring the needle through at C, 1 thread to the left of A.

Fig 2 From C, re-insert the needle at B and bring it out at D, 1 thread to the left of C.

Fig 3 Continue working stitches as shown, B-E, B-F, B-G, B-H, B-I.

Fig 4 This shows the completed Eyelet Hole.

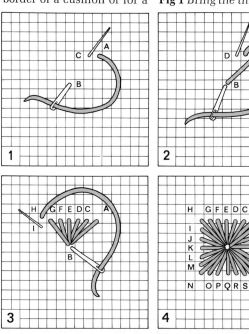

Mosaic ▶

Florentine Stitch, Single

This is used for working the wave or zigzag patterns popularly known as Florentine work. Straight stitches of the same length are worked over the horizontal threads of canvas, forming a wave or zigzag pattern. The size of the wave may be varied, depending on the number of threads over which the stitches are worked.

In the design on the opposite page, stitches are worked over 4 horizontal threads and a toning range of Tapisserie wool colours is used.

Fig 1 *Bring the thread through at A and insert the needle 4 threads above at B. The next stitch, C-D, is stepped 2 threads up, and so are E-F and G-H. Continue working across the row, stepping stitches as shown, I-J, K-L, M-N and so on.*

Fig 2 *The second row of stitches is worked over the same number of threads and the stitches are placed immediately below those of the first row.*

Fig 3 *This shows how the rows of stitches are worked in different colours. Row 3 uses colours 1 and 2, and colour 3 is introduced.*

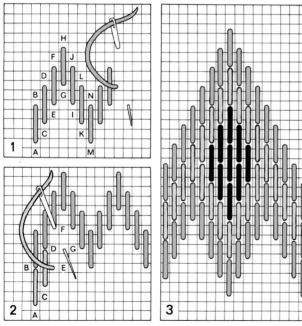

Florentine 1 ▶

A working chart for this design is on page 104

42

Florentine Stitch, Composite

Fig 1 Bring the thread through at A and insert the needle at B, 6 threads above. Bring the thread through at C, 1 thread to the right of A and insert the needle at D, 1 thread to the right of B. Work E-F over 6 threads to complete the block of 3 Straight stitches.

The second block of stitches is stepped up 3 threads (G-H, I-J, K-L, M-N), and the needle emerges at 0, 3 threads up ready to start the third block.

Fig 2 The second row is worked over the same number of threads and the blocks are placed immediately below those of the first row.

Fig 3 This shows an area of composite Florentine, worked over 6 threads but with a varying number of stitches in the blocks.

Florentine 2▶

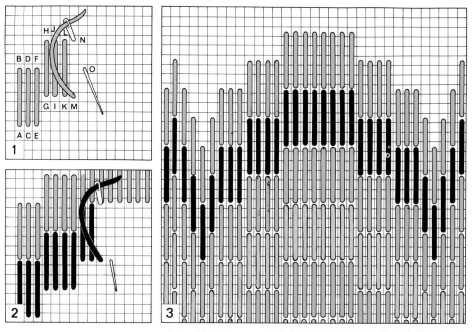

44

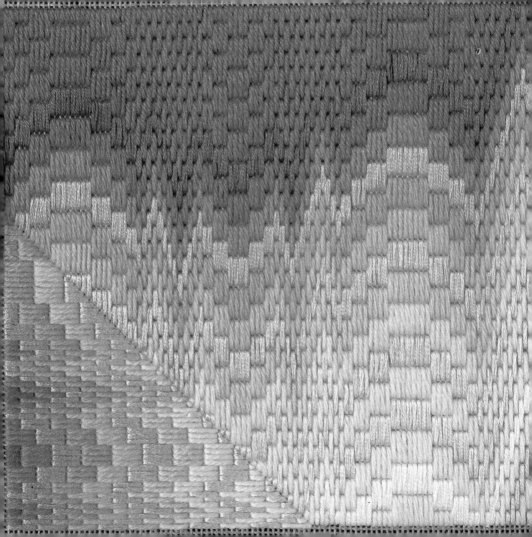

French Knots

Many knotted stitches can be adapted for canvas embroidery and French Knots are one of the simplest to work. They can be used in close rows for a textured area or used singly as in 'City Park' on the opposite page. Here, French Knots are worked to represent bright red, pink and yellow flowers, scattered round the lakeside and across the Chain Stitch foreground. Textural interest is provided by other stitches — Satin Stitch, Gobelin Filling, Cross Stitch, Long Satin Stitch and Brick Stitch. Tapisserie wool is used in the following colours: 8922, 9212, 9100, 9202, 9800, 9172, 9534, 9192, 8168 and 8454.

Fig 1 *Bring the thread through on the exact spot where the knot is required (A). Hold the thread between finger and thumb of the left hand and twist the needle once round it.*

Fig 2 *Tighten the twist of thread, then turn the point of the needle away from you and insert it at B, over 1 thread of canvas.*

Fig 3 *The finished Knots.*

City Park ▶
A working chart for this design is on page 105

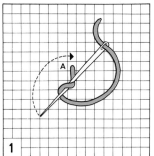

1

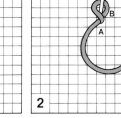

2

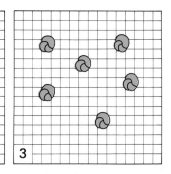

3

46

Gobelin Filling

The name Gobelin covers a range of Straight Stitch patterns which can be worked over differing numbers of threads and in a variety of combinations. This Filling is worked in rows, first from left to right, with spaces between the stitches, then from right to left, with the stitches fitting evenly into the previous row. The diagrams show the Filling worked over 6 horizontal threads. The spaces of the first and last row may be filled with Straight stitches worked over 3 threads.

The design opposite 'Landscape' is a detail from a larger picture and also uses Long Satin Stitch and Cross Stitches.

Fig 1 Bring the thread through at A and insert the needle at B 6 threads above, bringing the needle through at C, 2 threads to the right of A.

Fig 2 Continue to the end of the row, working Straight stitches C-D, E-F, G-H, I-J, leaving 2 threads between each stitch.

Fig 3 Working right to left, bring the needle through at K, 1 thread to the left and 3 threads below I. Insert the needle at L 6 threads above. Continue to the end of the row, K-L, M-N, O-P, Q-R, fitting stitches into the spaces in the previous row.

Fig 4 This shows the effect of 3 rows of Gobelin Filling. Fill the spaces on the first and last row with Straight Stitches worked over 3 threads.

Landscape ▶
A working chart for this design is on page 106

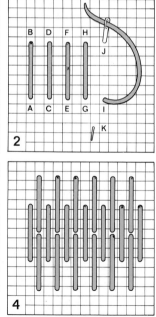

48

Double Gobelin Filling

In this variation, Straight Stitches are worked in groups of two with 3 threads left between groups. On the return row, groups of two stitches are worked in the spaces left in the previous row.

The design on the opposite page, 'Four Square', can be worked as a stitch sampler and framed for a picture, or four designs could be worked to make a square cushion cover. Worked on a coarser canvas with fewer threads to the measure, the design might be developed for a wall panel.

Tapisserie wool is used for 'Four Square' as follows: colour numbers 8776, 8774, 8914, 9502 and 8484.

Fig 1 Bring the thread through at A and insert the needle 6 threads up at B, bringing it out at C, 1 thread to the right of A.

Fig 2 From C, insert the needle at D, 6 threads up and 1 thread to the right of B, bringing the needle through at E, 3 threads to the right of C.

Fig 3 This shows 2 groups of stitches worked with 3 threads space between groups. Work I-J, then K-L. From L, bring the needle out at M, 3 threads below and 1 thread to the left of I.

Fig 4 Insert the needle at N, 6 threads above M. Continue, working right to left, fitting groups of 2 stitches into the spaces left in the previous row.

Four Square ▶
A working chart for this design is on page 107

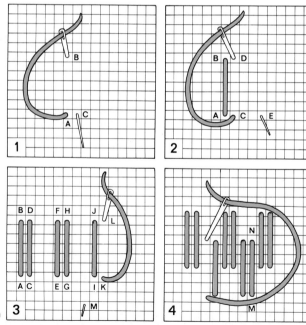

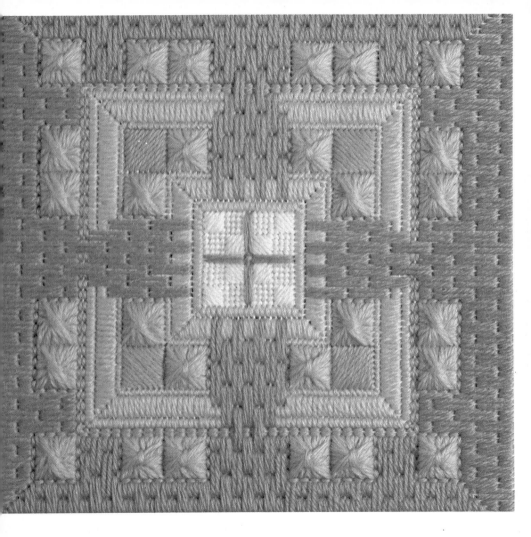

Straight Gobelin Stitch

There are two methods of working this stitch. When a very close, hardwearing effect is required, such as for a cushion or chair seat, work a Trammed Stitch first from left to right, then work Straight Stitches over the thread. In the second method, the laid thread is omitted. The effect is similar to the first but the stitch is not so hardwearing.

In the detail 'Rooftops' on the opposite page, Straight Gobelin has been used for the stone-coloured house wall, as well as in other areas of the embroidery.

Satin Stitch, Gobelin Filling and Cross Stitch are also used in the design. Tapisserie wool is used as follows: colour numbers 8306, 8264, 8302, 9524, 8104, 9776, 9656, 8006, 9274, 9212, 9214 and 9266.

Fig 1, Method 1 *Lay a thread from A to B over 8 vertical threads. From B, bring the needle through 1 thread down and 1 thread to the left at C. Insert the needle 2 threads above at D, bringing it out at E, 1 thread to the left of C.*

Fig 2 *Continue working rows in the same way.*

Fig 3, Method 2 *Bring the needle through at A and insert it at B, 2 threads above. Bring the needle through at C, 1 thread to the left of A, ready to work the second stitch.*

Fig 4 *Continue working rows of Straight Stitches in the same way.*

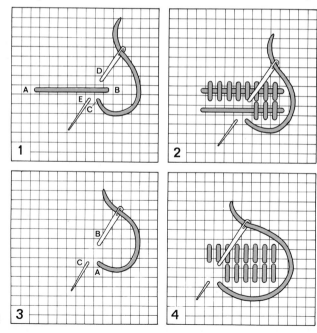

Rooftops ▶

Herringbone Multi-plait

This can be worked as a square or as a diamond shape. It creates an illusion of depth but although it looks difficult, the Herringbone Multi-plait is comparatively easy to work. The stitch starts with a Cross Stitch and then stitches are laid across and around the cross. (It helps to remember that the needle is coming through on odd numbers and is being inserted on even numbers.)

Herringbone Multi-plaits are used for the central area of the design 'Indian Diamond' on the opposite page. Satin Stitch worked both horizontally and vertically borders the area, with rows of Upright Cross Stitches worked between. Gobelin Filling is used for the ground area.

Fig 1 Work a Cross Stitch over 2 horizontal and 2 vertical threads. (1-2, 3-4). From 4, pass the needle through at 5, 1 thread to the left of 2.

Take the needle to position 6, 1 thread above the place the thread first came through. Bring it through at 7, 2 threads to the left of 6.

Fig 2 This shows the first stitch overlaid on the cross, with the second stitch, 7-8, being laid and the needle in position for stitch 9-10.

Fig 3 Follow the numbered diagram until 4 threads have been overlaid on all four sides of the diamond (see Fig 4).

Indian Diamond ▶
A working chart for this design is on page 108

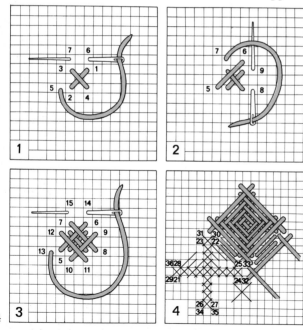

54

Herringbone Stitch, Variation

Herringbone is one of the stitches related to the cross stitch family. In this variation, the first row of stitches is worked from left to right, then the second row fits between the 'long arms' of the previous row. The result of massed rows can be seen in the sample opposite giving the effect of a woven fabric.

Related tones in Tapisserie wool are used to work the sample as follows: colour numbers 8588, 8590, 8604, 8608, 8610 and 8594.

Fig 1 Bring the thread through at A and insert the needle at B, 4 threads up and 4 to the right.

Bring the needle through at C, 2 threads to the left of B, and insert it again at D, 4 threads down and 4 threads to the right. Continue in the same way across the row, working D-E, E-F, F-G, G-H, H-I, I-J, J-K.

The second row is worked right to left as follows; from K, insert the needle at L, 4 threads down and 4 threads to the right. Bring the needle out at M, 2 threads below L.

Fig 2 From M, insert the needle at N, 4 threads up and 4 threads to the left, bringing it out at O, 2 threads to the right.

Fig 3 From O, insert the needle at P, 4 threads down and 4 threads to the left, bringing it out at Q, 2 threads to the right. Continue across the row (see Fig 4).

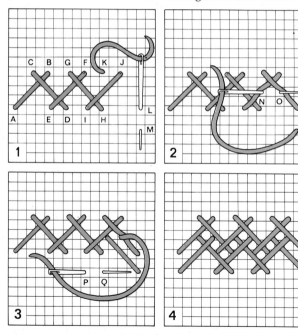

Horizontal ▶

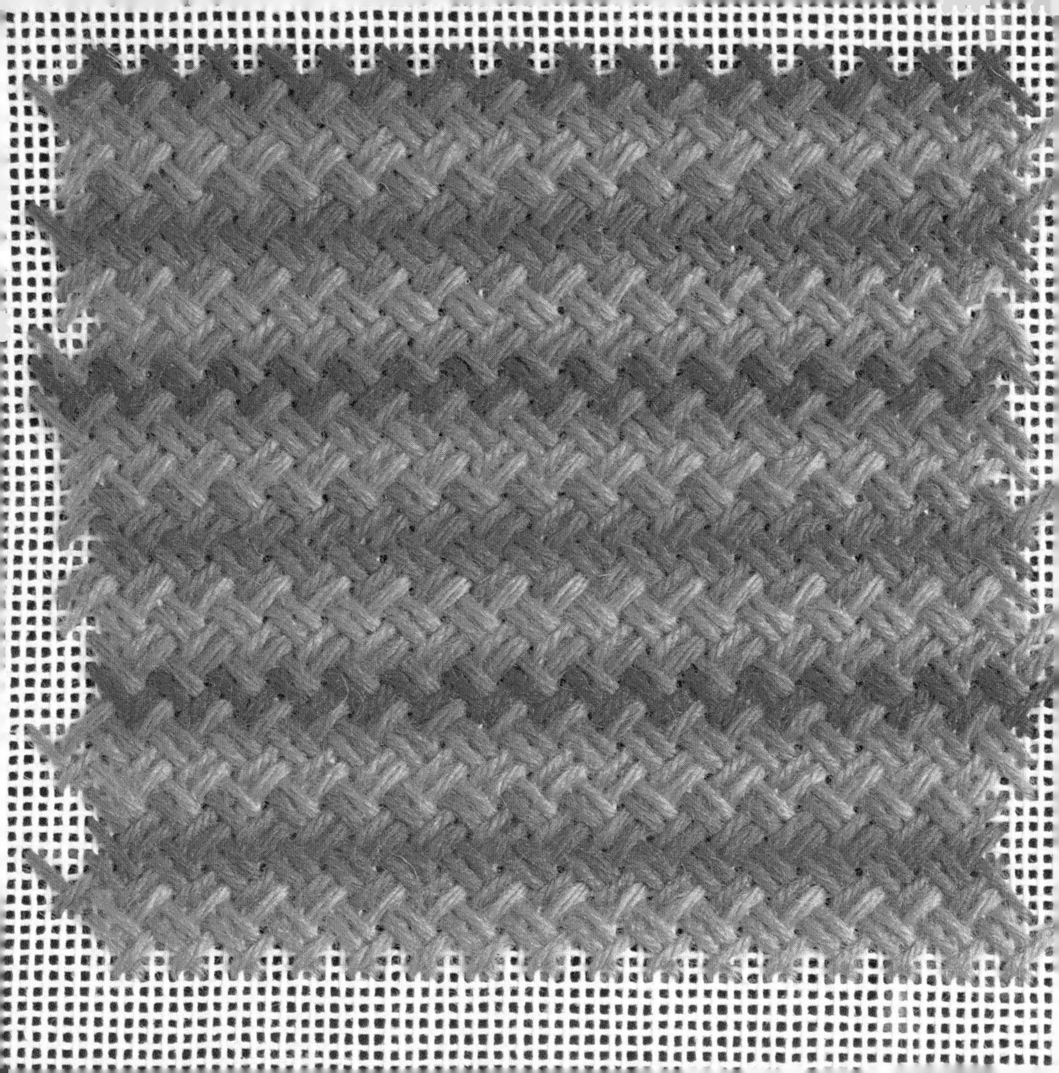

Hungarian Stitch

This can be worked in one colour as the wide border in the design 'Cerise Square' opposite or in two, depending on the effect required. It makes a close, even texture and is ideal for working large areas where a woven fabric effect is required. You can also use it for adding interesting texture to a design where there may be large areas of Long Satin Stitch or similar regular stitches.

The stitch consists of rows of vertical Straight stitches worked in sequence over 2, 4 and 2 threads of canvas, leaving 2 vertical threads between groups of stitches. Each row is set alternately into the preceding row as shown in Fig. 3.

Tapisserie wool is used to work the 'Cerise Square' as follows: colour numbers 8488, 8490, 8528, 8552 and 8484.

Fig 1 Working right to left, bring the thread through at A and insert it at B, 2 threads above. Bring the needle through at C, 1 thread below and 1 thread to the left of A and insert it at D, 4 threads above. Work E-F, then leave a 2-thread space. Work G-H, I-J and continue across the row in the same way.

Fig 2 This shows the row being completed.

Fig 3 The second row is worked left to right and is set alternately into the space left between the groups of stitches.

Fig 4 This shows the effect of 4 rows with the fifth row being worked.

Cerise Square ▶
A working chart for this design is on page 109

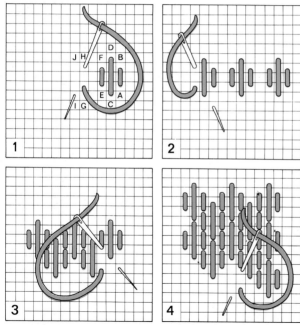

58

Hungarian Stitch Variation

This is another variation on a versatile stitch and in this instance, vertical Straight stitches are worked in sequence over 2, 4, 6 and 4 horizontal threads of canvas. Each row is set alternately into the preceding row, pro-ducing a close textured effect, rather like a woven fabric.

The design on the oppo-site page 'Flower Abstract' uses several stitches be-sides Hungarian Stitch Variation — Gobelin Fill-ing, Petit Point, Cross Stitch and Satin Stitch.

Fig 1 Working right to left, bring the thread through at A and insert the needle at B, 2 threads above. Bring the needle through at C, 3 threads down and 1 to the left, and insert it at D, 4 threads up. Bring the needle through at E 5 threads down and 1 thread to the left and insert it at F 6 threads above. Complete the sequence to the end of the row (Fig 2).

Fig 3 Working left to right, bring the thread through 6 threads below the last short stitch of the previous row. Insert the needle 6 threads up and bring it through 5 threads down and 1 thread to the right. Continue, setting stitches into the preceding row.

Fig 4 The effect of 3 rows of Hungarian Stitch Variation.

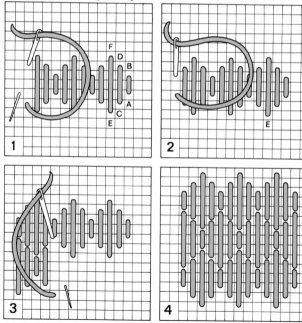

Flower Abstract ▶

Jacquard Stitch

This interesting stitch produces a woven fabric or brocaded effect when worked over large areas.

Rows of stitches are worked diagonally from upper left to lower right and each row is completed before starting the next. The length of stitches alternates, in one row the stitches are worked diagonally over 2 canvas thread intersections, and in the next row over 1 canvas thread intersection.

Fig 1, Work diagonal Straight Stitches over 2 thread intersections as shown and follow the broken lines and arrows for positioning stitches.

Fig 2 The second row of diagonal Straight Stitches is worked over 1 thread intersection.

Fig 3, This shows the effect of 6 rows of Jacquard Stitch.

Jacquard ▶
A working chart for this design is on page 110

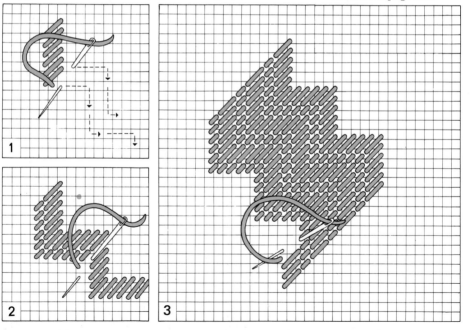

Laid Oriental Stitch

This stitch is also known as Roumanian Couching and produces a most attractive texture and a firm fabric. It has been used for the sea in the design 'Storm', opposite and is ideally suited for the effect that is required here. Three Tapisserie wool colours are used — 8918, 8938, 8914. Stranded Cotton is used for the sky.

Apart from the Laid Oriental foreground, the entire design is worked in Long Satin Stitch.

Fig 1 Bring the thread through at the top left corner of the area to be worked (A) and insert the needle at B (right) so that the yarn lies between 2 horizontal threads of canvas. Bring the needle through at C, 2 threads to the left and immediately below the laid thread. Take the working thread over the laid thread and insert the needle at D, 6 vertical threads to the left, bringing it out 1 vertical thread of canvas to the left at E.

Fig 2 Continue the process of couching to the end of the laid thread.

Fig 3 This shows the effect of close rows of Laid Oriental.

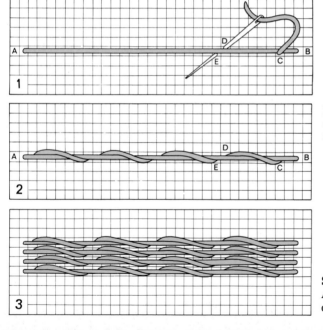

Storm ▶
A working chart for this design is on page 111

64

Leaf Stitch

To achieve the effect of a leaf, stitches are set diagonally left and right from the centre. In the Autumn design opposite, Leaf Stitches are worked in toning shades on the borders, each leaf fitting into the previous row.

Fig 1 *Bring the needle through at A and insert at B, 3 threads to the left and 4 threads above. Work C-D and E-F, parallel to A-B. Then, bringing the thread through at G, insert the needle at H, 1 thread above and 1 to the right of F, bringing it out at I, 1 thread above G.*

Fig 2 *For the next stitch, the needle is inserted at J, 1 thread above and 1 to the right of H, and then the thread is brought out at K, 2 threads above I. The centre stitch, K-L, is worked over 3 horizontal threads.*

Bring the needle through at I again and insert the needle at M, 4 threads up and 1 to the right. Bring the needle through at G again and insert it at N, 4 threads up and 2 to the right.

Complete the leaf, working E-O, C-P, A-Q, to match the other side.

Fig 3 *When the last stitch of the leaf has been worked, (Q), bring the thread through at R, 4 threads down and 3 to the right ready to work the second leaf stitch.*

Fig 4 *For a variation, work a single Long stitch along the centre of the leaf.*

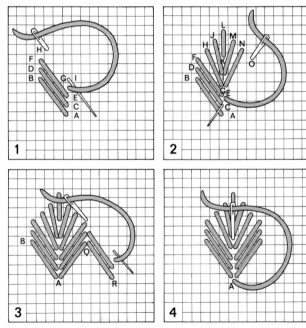

Autumn ▶
A working chart for this design is on page 112

66

Long Satin Stitch

This is one of the easiest stitches to work and is popular with beginners. It is also quick to work and, when mixed with other stitches, attractive designs can be developed. Long Satin Stitch, when used extensively in a design, is not suitable for cushion covers as the long threads tend to catch. It is better kept for pictures and wall hangings.

The design on the opposite page 'Beached Boats' is a detail from a larger picture but is an interesting exercise in working Long Satin Stitch. Stem Stitch has been used for the ropes and Satin Stitches worked in a chevron pattern have been used for the background.

Long Satin Stitches can be worked over any number of canvas threads to fill a design area.

The stitch is illustrated in the diagrams worked over varying numbers of horizontal threads.

Fig 1 *Bring the thread through at A and insert the needle at B, 10 threads above. Bring the needle through again at C, 1 thread to the right of A.*

Fig 2 *Insert the needle at D, 11 threads up and bring it through again at E, 1 thread to the right and 3 threads above C. Insert the needle again at F, level with D. Bring it through at G 1 thread to the right and 1 thread below E.*

Fig 3 *Continue working Long Satin Stitches in the same way working over the number of horizontal threads required to fill the design area.*

Beached Boats ▶
A trace-off pattern for this design is on page 113

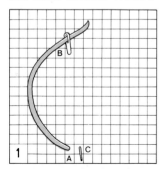

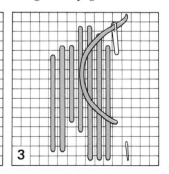

68

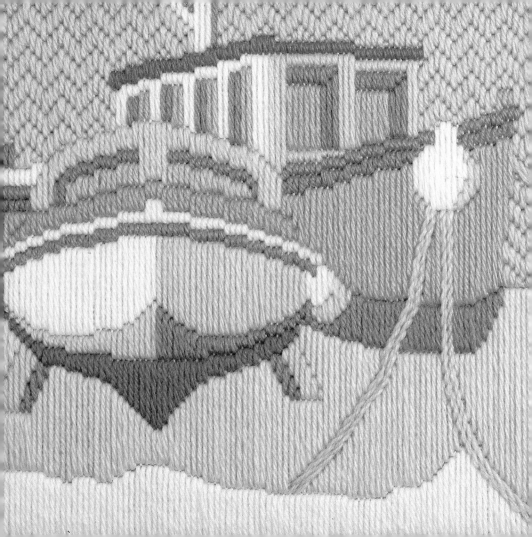

Norwich Stitch

This is also known as Southern Cross and has the appearance of a raised diamond on a square base. Although it looks complex it is in fact easy to work. Just remember when working from the diagrams, to bring your needle up on the odd numbers and pass it down on the even numbers.

Fig 1 *Bring the thread through at 1, insert the needle at 2, 9 threads up and 9 diagonal intersections up to the right, bringing it through again at 3, 9 threads down and level with 1.*

Fig 2 *Make a diagonal stitch across to 4, then bring the needle through at 5, 1 thread to the left of 2.*

Fig 3 *From 5, insert the needle at 6, 1 thread above 1 and bring it through at 7, 1 thread below 4.*

Fig 4 *Shows the continued construction of the stitch.*

Fig 5 *When the last stitch is put in (35-36), the needle is slipped under instead of over stitch 29-30, and the needle then passes into the canvas at 36.*

Crosses and Squares ▶
A working chart for this design is on page 114

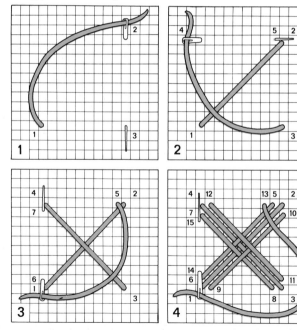

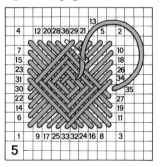

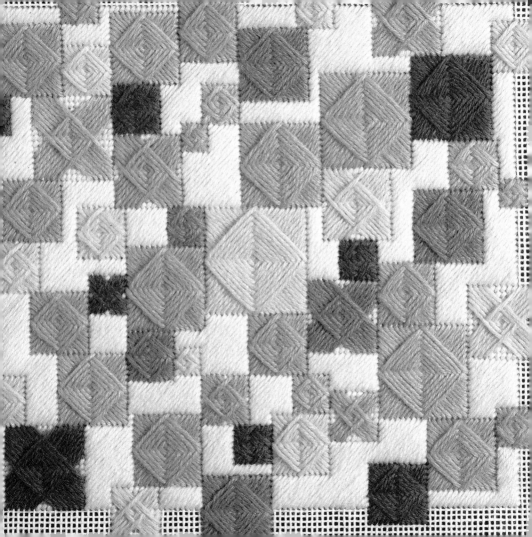

Parisian Stitch

This is one of the Straight Stitches and forms a close texture over the canvas. Stitches in each row alternate from one short stitch to one long stitch. Work left to right, then right to left so that the tops of the short stitches are in the same canvas holes as the bases of the long stitches in the preceding row (see Fig 3).

Parisian Stitch is used for the centres of the green diamonds in the design on the opposite page, and for the chevron-shaped areas at the corners.

Stranded Cotton is used to work 'Green Diamonds'

Fig 1 *Working left to right, bring the thread through at A and insert the needle at B 6 threads above, bringing the needle through at C, 4 threads down and 1 thread to the right.*

Fig 2 *To make the short stitch, from C, insert the needle at D 2 threads above. Bring the needle through at E, 4 threads down and 1 thread to the right, ready to make the next long stitch.*

Fig 3 *Continue to the end of the row, then, working right to left, work short stitch G-E, and bring the needle through at H, 2 threads below G and 1 thread to the left. The needle will be inserted at C to complete the long stitch.*

Fig 4 *Shows the effect of Parisian Stitch with the third row being worked.*

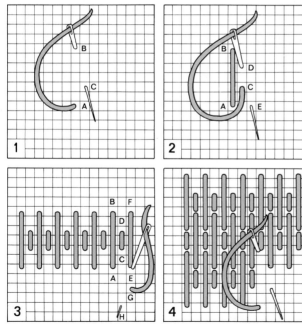

Green Diamonds ▶
A working chart for this design is on page 115

Pinwheel Milanese

This attractive stitch is formed by working triangles of Straight stitches around a central point as shown in the sample 'Pinwheels' on the opposite page.

Fig 1 *To form the first triangle, bring the thread through at 1 and insert the needle 15 threads to the right at 2, bringing it out at 3, 14 threads to the left and 1 thread up. Continue forming parallel stitches, 2 threads shorter each time until the triangle is completed on stitch 15-16.*

Fig 2 *From 16, bring the thread through at 17, 3*

threads up and 3 to the left. Insert the needle at 2 again work stitch 2-18, then 18-19, 20-21 etc, until the triangle is completed on stitch 34-35.

Fig 3 *shows the completed Pinwheel Milanese with eight triangles set around the centre point.*

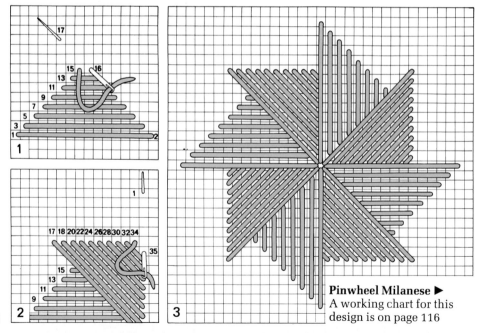

Pinwheel Milanese ▶
A working chart for this design is on page 116

74

Plait Stitch

The detail on the opposite page, 'House in the Trees' shows Plait Stitch used for the roof of the house and this is a good example of how stitches can be used to depict an area in pictorial design. Long Satin Stitch is used for the fields, trees and house walls, with Chain Stitch outlining the windows and doors. Petit Point Stitches detail the windows and French Knots are massed for foliage. Cross Stitches provide texture in the fields.

Tapisserie wool is used to work this design as follows: colour numbers 9172, 9162, 9204, 9560, 9452, 9390, 9214, 9450, 8686, 9662 and 9534.

Fig 1 *Bring the thread through at A and insert it at B, 4 diagonal intersections up to the right. Bring the needle through at C 4 threads below B.*

Fig 2 *From C, insert the needle at D, 2 threads to the left of B, and bring it through at E, 4 threads down.*

Fig 3 *From E, insert the needle at F, 4 diagonal intersections up to the right and bring the needle through at G, 4 threads below.*

Fig 4 *Shows the effect of Plait Stitch.*

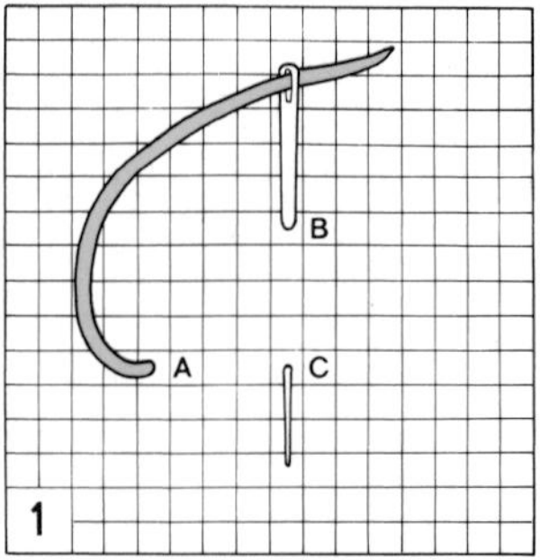

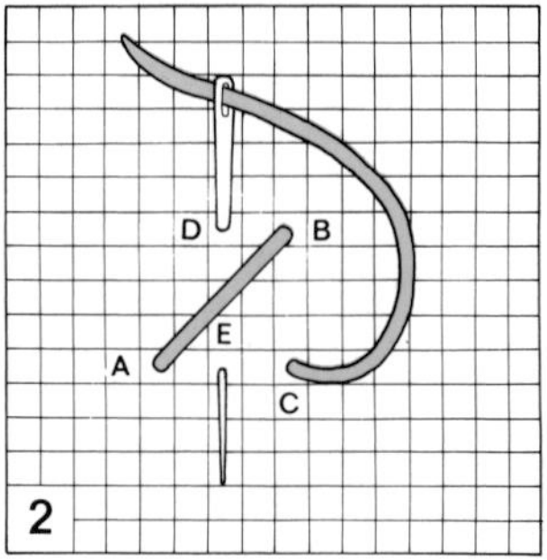

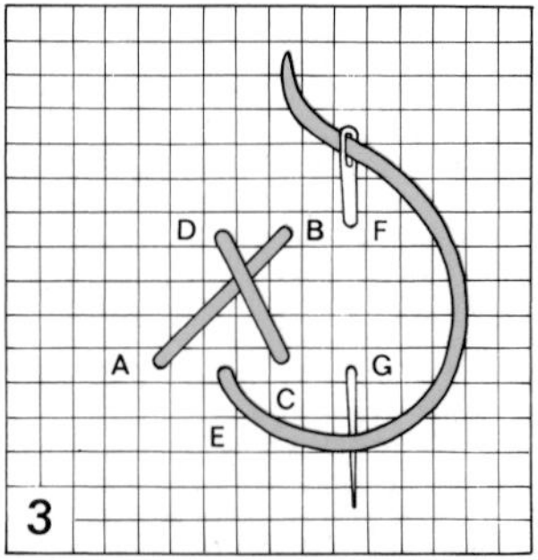

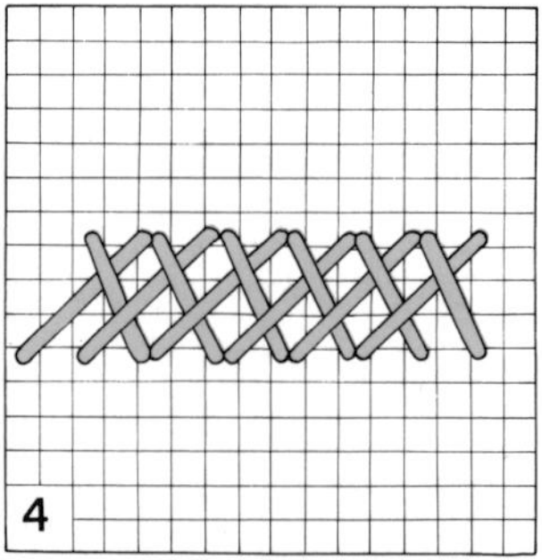

House in the Trees ▶
A trace-off pattern for this design on page 117

76

Rhodes Stitch

This chunky stitch was invented by a British needle-work designer, Mary Rhodes. It is a square stitch which may be worked over any area of canvas from three to twenty-four horizontal and vertical threads of canvas.

In the sample opposite 'Tile Pattern', Rhodes Stitches are worked over eleven horizontal and vertical threads. In the diagrams, the stitch is demonstrated over six horizontal and vertical threads.

A limited range of colours is used in 'Tile Pattern' — Tapisserie wool colour numbers 9252 and 9254, and Stranded Cotton in colour numbers 0842 and 0213. The interest in the design is provided by the contrasting textures of smooth Satin Stitches. Double Cross Stitches and the bulky Rhodes Stitches.

Fig 1 *Bring the thread through at A and insert the needle at B in the opposite corner of the design square. Bring the needle through at C, 1 thread to the right of A. From C, insert the needle at D.*

Fig 2 *Continue round the square, moving in the same direction, E-F, G-H, I-J.*

Fig 3 *Continue working in the same way until stitches passing across the centre of the square have been worked into every hole around the edge.*

Fig 4 *A small stitch can be used to tie Rhodes Stitch down in the centre.*

Tile Pattern ▶
A working chart for this design is on page 118

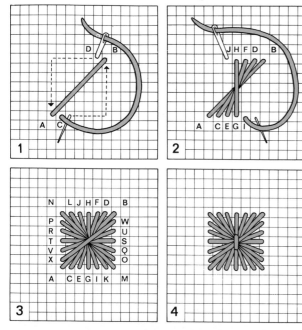

Rhodes Stitch, Half Drop

The Half Drop Variation is simply half a Rhodes Stitch. The effect can be seen in the diamond shape in the middle of the border detail on the opposite page. Four Tapisserie wool colours are used for the stitch in this area and it is repeated on the border edges, worked over long Satin Stitches.

The effectiveness of the design, which could be repeated to edge a large cushion, or used for curtain tiebacks, is achieved by the limited range of closely related colour. Tapisserie wool is used as follows: colour numbers 9532, 9556, 9522, 9554 and 9552.

Fig 1 Bring the thread through at A and insert it at B on the opposite corner of the design square. Bring the needle through at C, 1 thread to the right of A.

Fig 2 Work C-D, E-F, G-H, bringing the needle through at I, ready to work I-J.

Fig 3 When the opposite diagonal is reached (M-N), the Half Drop is completed.

Fig 4 From N, bring the thread through at O, 3 threads below I and insert it at P, 6 diagonal intersections up to the right. Bring the thread through at Q, 1 thread to the right of O, inserting the needle at R, 1 thread to the left of P. Continue working S-T etc until the opposite diagonal has been reached (as Fig 3).

Border ▶
A working chart for this design is on page 119

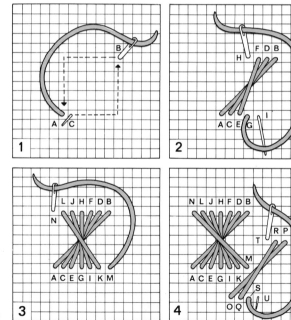

80

Rhodes Octagonal

When the Rhodes Stitch is worked over an octagonal area instead of a square, the stitch becomes even chunkier. Used with smaller Rhodes Stitches, an attractive textured pattern is achieved. This combination of stitches could be used on wall panels and in pictures, as well as being useful for a variety of home and fashion accessories.

Tapisserie wool is used for the design opposite entitled 'Amethyst', as follows: colour numbers 8588, 8522 and 8546.

Rhodes Octagonal can only be worked over a multiple of four canvas threads.

Fig 1 *This shows the formation of the stitch worked over 16 canvas threads for the first stage then over 14, 12, 10 and 8 threads for the second segment of the octagon. The third segment is over 16 threads, and the fourth over 14, 12, 10 and 8 threads, and so on.*

Fig 2 *Shows the sequence of stitches worked round the octagon shape to complete the Rhodes Octagon.*

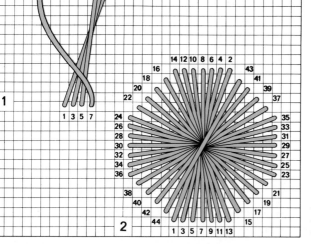

Amethyst▶
A working chart for this design is on page 120

82

Rice Stitch

8804, 8818, 8814.

This square stitch is begun with a diagonal Cross Stitch worked over an even number of canvas threads. Then a Back Stitch is worked over each arm of the Cross. In the sample on the opposite page, Rice Stitches are worked in a single colour in the centre of the design. Around the central square, the stitch is worked in two colours. When two colours are being worked, work the basic Cross Stitches first, then add the Back Stitches in the second colour afterwards.

Tapisserie wool is used for the embroidery as follows: colour numbers 8820,

Fig 1 *Work a diagonal Cross Stitch first over 4 horizontal and 4 vertical threads. For the second stage, bring the thread through at A and insert the needle at B, 2 diagonal intersections down to the right. Bring the needle through at C, 2 diagonal intersections down to the left.*

Fig 2 *Work C-B, B-D, D-A, A-D, D-C. From C of the second Cross, bring the needle out at A ready to work the third Cross.*

Fig 3 *Shows two rows of large Crosses worked to form Rice Stitch.*

Blue Tile ▶
A working chart for this design is on page 121

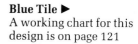

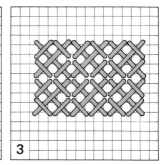

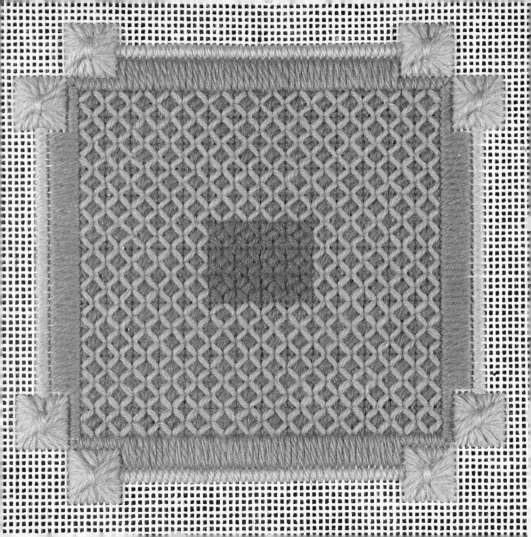

Rya Stitch

This is one of the pile stitches and produces a texture that stands away from the canvas. The stitch is worked as a series of loops which are cut afterwards to form the pile.

Fig 1 Begin at the lower left of the design and work rows left to right. Hold the thread end on the right side of the canvas (A) and pass the needle under 1 vertical canvas thread (A-B). Curve the excess thread up and pass the needle under the next vertical thread (C-A) and pull the thread through.

Fig 2 Holding the loop of thread to the desired length, pass the needle under the next vertical thread (D-C).

Fig 3 Still holding the loop, curve the thread up and pass the needle under the next vertical thread (E-D) and pull through. Continue across the row.

Fig 4 Work the stitches of the next row over the first row.

Fig 5 Cut the loops.

Rya ▶
A working chart for this design is on page 122

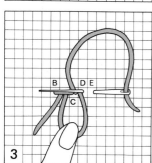

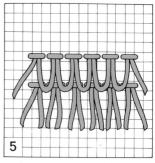

Satin Stitch

Satin Stitch is comprised of Straight Stitches set close together to cover the background fabric. They can be worked over varying numbers of threads and set vertically, horizontally or diagonally.

In the design 'Corner Piece' on the opposite page, Satin Stitches in different coloured Tapisserie wools form most of the pattern with Rhodes Stitches providing textural contrast.

The design would make an attractive cushion, repeated on the four corners, or the outer border might be worked round a mirror frame or picture frame.

Tapisserie wool colours are as follows: 9594, 8254, 8434, 8482 and 8484.

Fig 1 *To work Satin Stitches vertically, bring the thread through at A, insert the needle at B, 6 threads above and bring the needle through at C, 1 thread to the right of A.*

Fig 2 *Set stitches over the same number of canvas threads 1 thread apart.*

Fig 3 *Work stitches in the same way over vertical threads for horizontal Satin Stitches.*

Fig 4 *Diagonal Satin Stitches worked over 6 diagonal canvas thread intersections.*

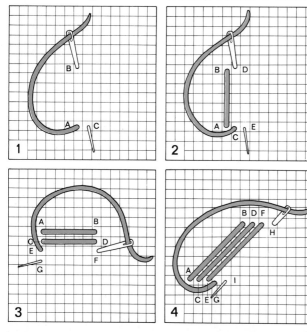

Corner Piece ▶
A working chart for this design is on page 123

Scottish Stitch

This square stitch consists of diagonal stitches worked over a sequence of one, two, three, four, three, two and one intersections of canvas. The cushions which are formed are worked in rows horizontally and are then edged with a row of Tent Stitch.

In the sample 'Stained Glass' on the opposite page, seven Tapisserie wool colours are used to produce the bright effect, with black Tent Stitches worked between the cushions in the central area. On the outer edges of the sample, the canvas threads are allowed to show between the cushions.

The following Tapisserie wool colours are used: 8692, 8608, 8588, 8488, 8458, 9100, 9096 and 9800.

Fig 1 *Bring the thread through at top left of the square and work A-B over 1 diagonal intersection of canvas. Bring the thread through at C and work C-D over 2 diagonal intersections. E-F is worked over 3 intersections, G-H is worked over 4 intersections. Continue working I-J, K-L, M-N, to complete the cushion.*

Fig 2 *Shows the fourth cushion being worked. One thread of canvas has been left between cushions.*

Fig 3 *Work Tent Stitches over 1 vertical and 1 horizontal thread round the cushion edges.*

Stained Glass ▶
A working chart for this design is on page 124

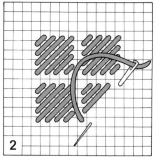

1

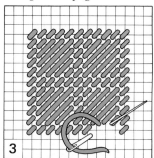

2

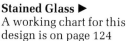

3

Split Stitch

'Harbour', the picture on the opposite page, is an ideal project for a beginner, using only three stitches, Satin Stitch, Cross Stitch and Split Stitch.

Split Stitch, which has been used for the building walls, the sail and the dock side is worked like Stem Stitch except that when the needle comes through it splits the working thread.

Tapisserie wool is used for the design as follows: colour numbers 9074, 8782, 8104, 8004, 8054, 9368, 8628, 8792 and 9452.

Fig 1 Bring the thread through at A at the left and insert the needle at B, 7 threads to the right.

Fig 2 Bring the needle through at C, 1 thread to the left of B, through the centre of the laid thread.

Fig 3 From C, insert the needle at D, 6 threads to the right.

Fig 4 For the second row, bring the thread through at E, 1 thread down and 3 threads to the left. Insert the needle at F, 5 threads to the right and bring it through 1 thread to the right of E, in the centre of the laid thread. Insert the needle at G, 7 threads to the left of E. Continue across the row.

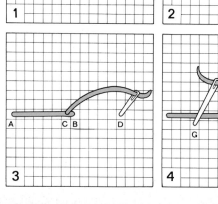

Harbour▶
A working chart for this design is on page 125

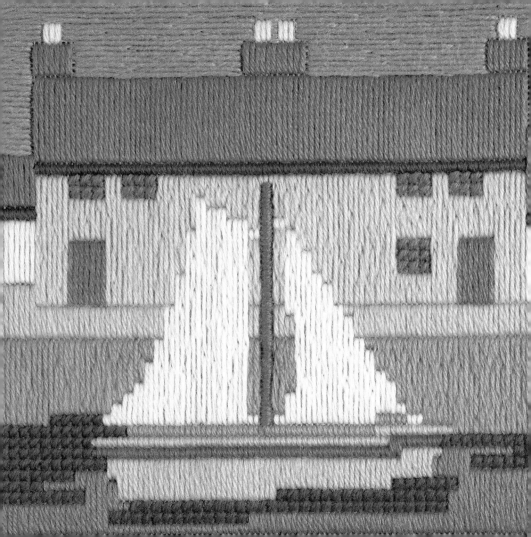

Tent Stitch

Figs 1-4 *show the methods for working Tent Stitch diagonally downwards (1), diagonally upwards (2), right to left (3) and left to right (4). Tent Stitches are worked over 1 diagonal intersection of canvas thread.*

Tramming: *For a hardwearing fabric, Tent Stitches can be worked over a laid thread on double thread canvas.*
Fig 5 *To lay the thread, bring it through at A on the left and insert the needle at B 7 double threads to the right. Bring the thread through at C, 1 double thread down and 1 to the*

left. Insert the needle at D, 1 diagonal intersection to the right to set the first Tent Stitch.

Fig 6 *Continue working Tent Stitches over the laid thread.*

Trellis ▶
A working chart for this design is on page 126

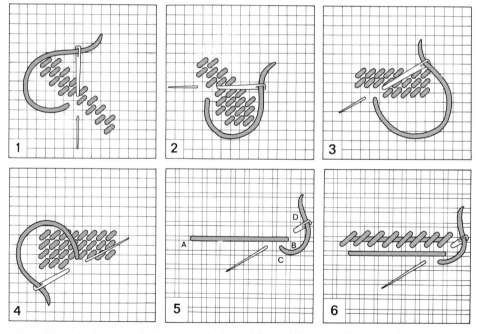

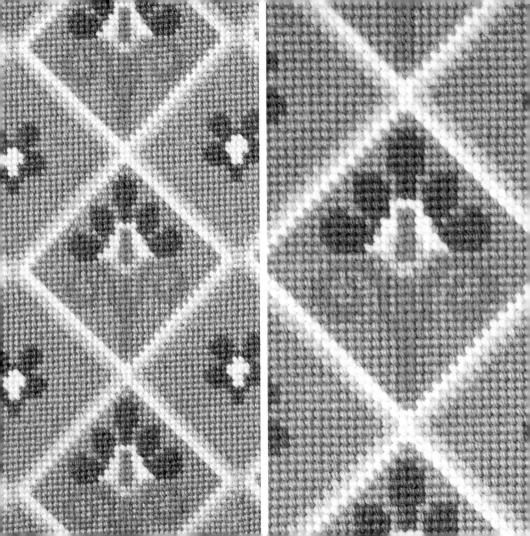

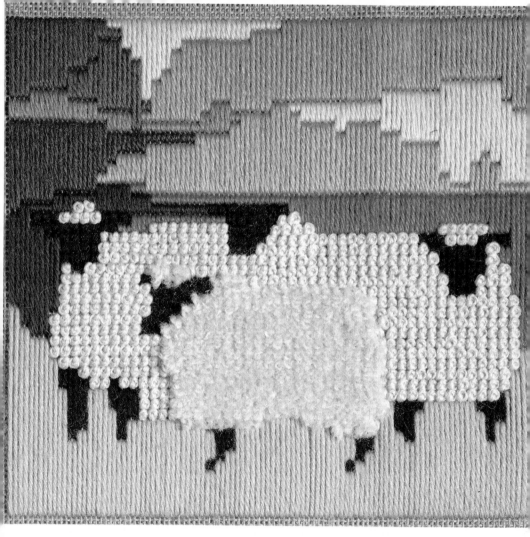

Velvet Stitch

Velvet Stitch is another of the pile stitches and, although it is usually used for making rugs it is suitable for areas of canvaswork where a pile effect is required such as on the sheep in the detail opposite.

Fig 1 Begin at lower left and work left to right. Bring thread through at A and insert the needle at B, 2 diagonal intersections up to the right, bringing the needle through again at A. From A, hold the loop of thread with the thumb and re-insert the needle at B, bringing it out at C, 2 threads down, with the needle point under the thread.

Fig 2 Pass the needle back over 2 diagonal intersections to the left and insert the needle at D, bringing it out again at C.

Fig 3 From C, insert the needle at E, 2 diagonal intersections up to the right, bringing the needle through again at C.

Fig 4 Continue working Velvet Stitches left to right.

Fig 5 Shows three rows of Velvet Stitches worked. Cut the loops by sliding the scissors blade through.

◄ **Sheep**

A working chart for this design is on page 127

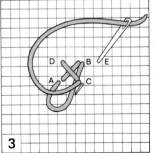

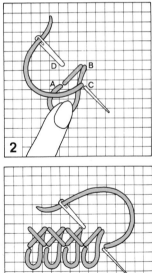

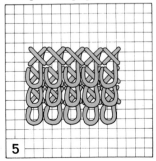

97

Red Ship page 5 **Key:** *A and B colour 8420, C = 8530, D = 8524, E, F and G = 8672, H and I = 8924, J and K = 8818, L and M = 8920, N, O, P and Q = 8914, R and S = 8004, T and U = 8456, V and W = 8212*

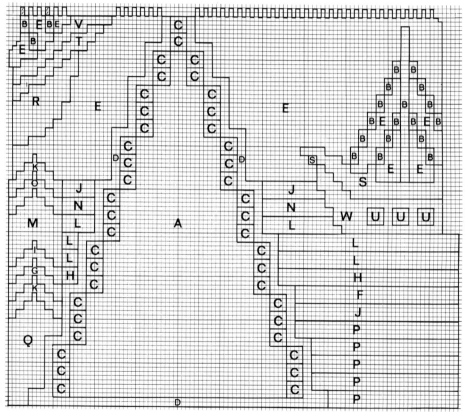

Diamonds page 9 **Key:** *A = colour 8454, B = 8456, C = 8510, D = 8506, E = 8504, F = 8302* ▶

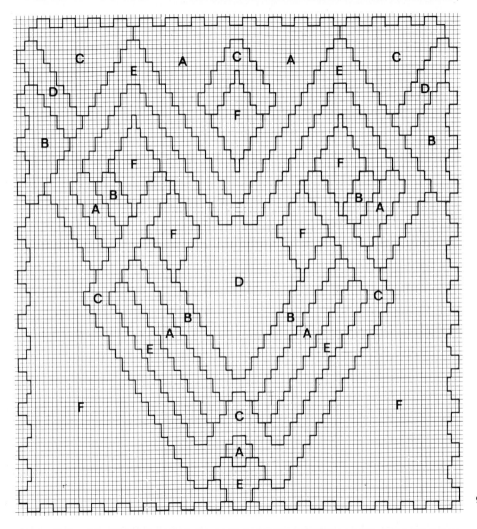

99

Squares and Zigzags page 21 **Key:** *A and C = 8004, B and G = 9488, D = 9522, E = 9442, F = 9554, H = 8872, I = 8772, J = 3734*

Pansy page 23 **Key:** *A = 8604, B and C = 8608, D = 8524, E = 8302*

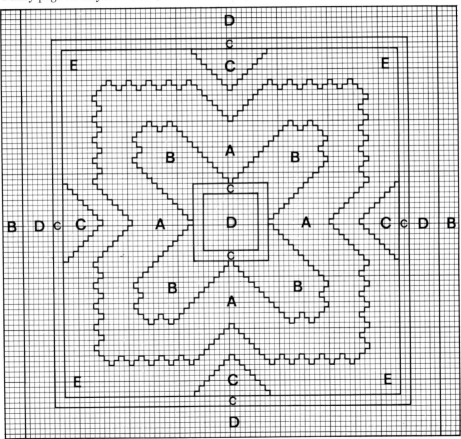

Brocade page 37 **Key:** *A = colour 8922, B = 8920, C = 8918, D = 8934, E = 8914*

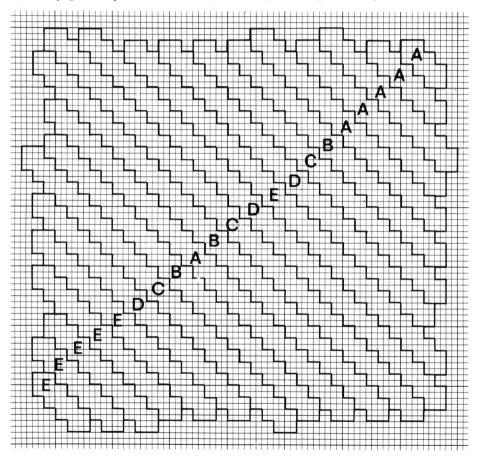

Butterfly front cover

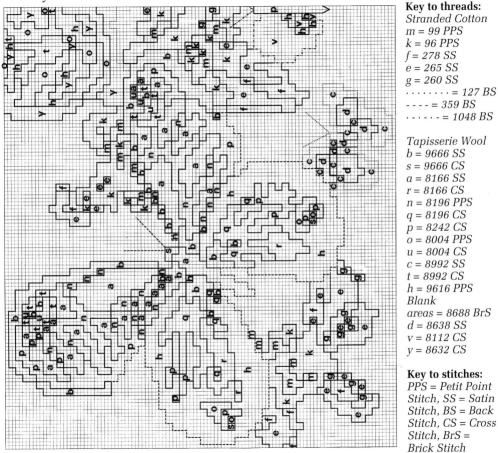

Key to threads:

Stranded Cotton
m = 99 PPS
k = 96 PPS
f = 278 SS
e = 265 SS
g = 260 SS
⋯⋯⋯ = 127 BS
- - - - = 359 BS
· - · - · - = 1048 BS

Tapisserie Wool
b = 9666 SS
s = 9666 CS
a = 8166 SS
r = 8166 CS
n = 8196 PPS
q = 8196 CS
p = 8242 CS
o = 8004 PPS
u = 8004 CS
c = 8992 SS
t = 8992 CS
h = 9616 PPS
Blank
areas = 8688 BrS
d = 8638 SS
v = 8112 CS
y = 8632 CS

Key to stitches:
PPS = Petit Point
Stitch, SS = Satin
Stitch, BS = Back
Stitch, CS = Cross
Stitch, BrS =
Brick Stitch

103

Florentine page 43   *colours 8040, 8042, 9204, 9174, 9164, 9212, 9192, 8036, 8038*

City Park page 47 **Key:** *A = colour 8922, a = 9100, B = 9212, C = 9202, D = 9800, E = 9172, F = 9534, G = 9192, H = 8168, I = 8454, J = 8644*

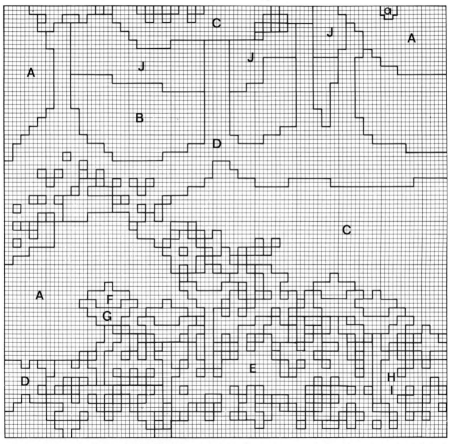

105

Landscape page 49 **Key:** *A = colour 8034, B = 9522, C = 9532, D = 9554, E = 9560, F = 9556 and 9560, G = 8106, H = 9396*

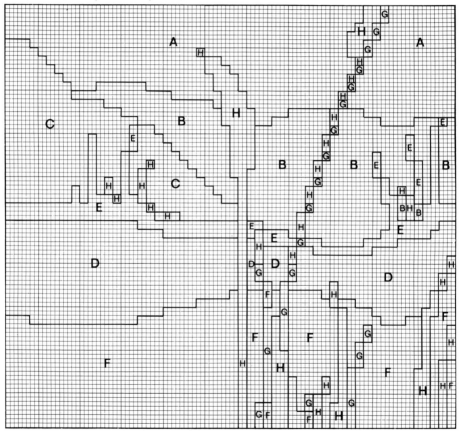

Four Square page 51 **Key:** *A and B = colour 8776, C = 8774, D = 8484, E = 8914, F = 9502* ▶

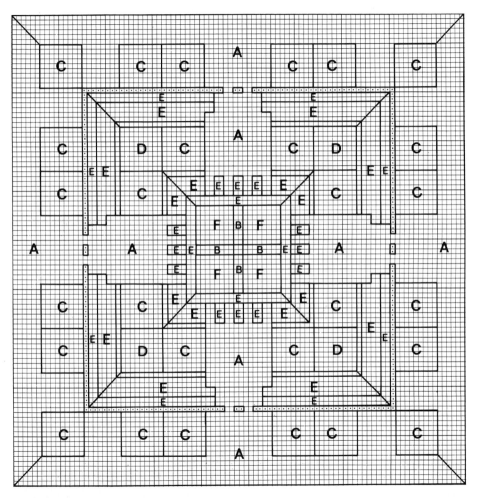

Cerise Square page 59 **Key:** *A = colour 8488, B = 8484, C = 8490, D = 8528, E = 8552*

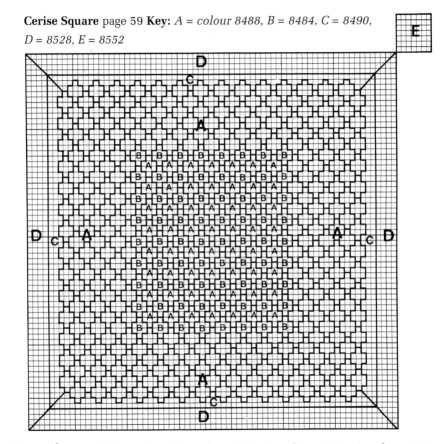

◀ **Indian Diamond** page 55 **Key:** *A and B = colour 8542, C and D = 8706, E and F = 8004, G and H = 8396*

Jacquard page 63 **Key:** *A = colour 8434, B = 8400*

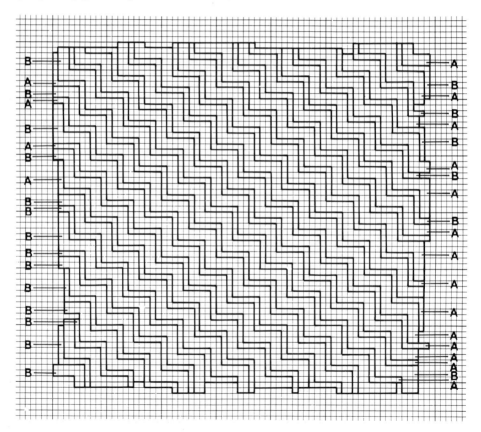

Storm page 65 **Key:** *A = colour 8938, B = 8918, C = 8914, D = (Stranded Cotton) 0847, E = 8624, F = 8522, G = 8342, H = 9324, I = 9384, J = 9372, K = 8004*

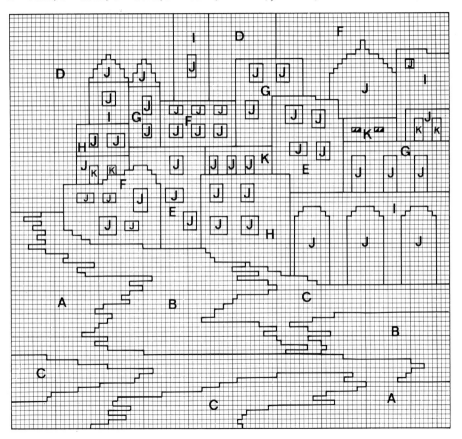

Leaf Border page 67 **Key:** *A = colour 9406, B and D = 9404, C, E and G = 8054, F = 8036*

Beached Boats page 69. *To use this design, place the pattern under the canvas and trace the lines using a waterproof pen.*

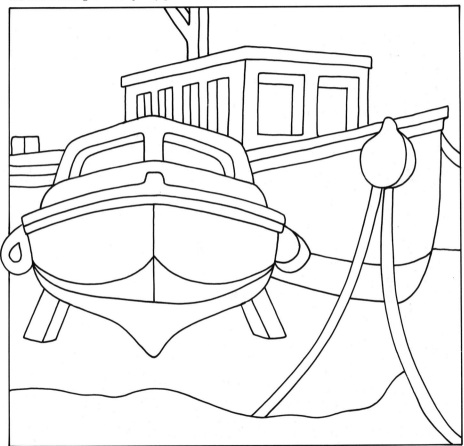

Crosses and Squares page 71 **Key:** *A = colour 8872, B = 8804, C = 8934, D = 8874, E = 8876, F = 8882, G = 8034*

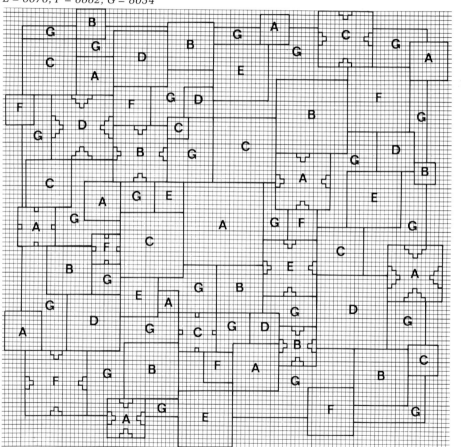

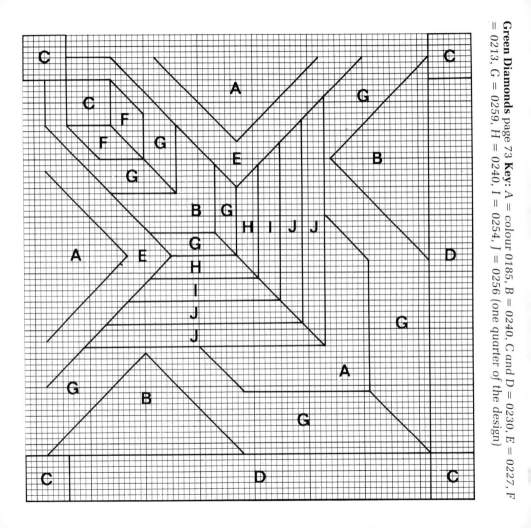

Green Diamonds page 73 **Key:** A = colour 0185, B = 0240, C and D = 0230, E = 0227, F = 0213, G = 0259, H = 0240, I = 0254, J = 0256 (one quarter of the design)

Pinwheel Milanese page 75 **Key:** *A and B = colour 8308, C = 8324, D = 9554, E = 9552, F = 8342*

House in the Trees page 77. To use this design, place the pattern under the canvas and trace the lines using a waterproof pen. Choose your own colour scheme.

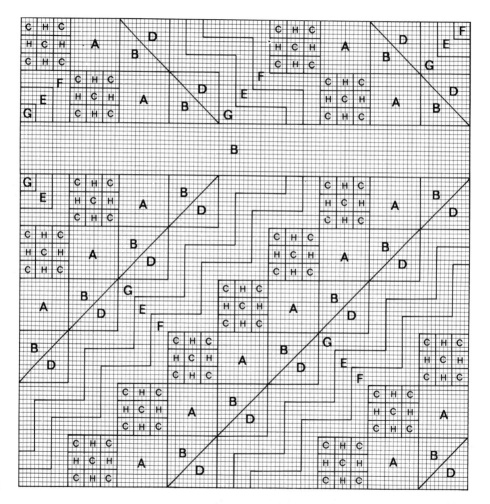

Border page 81 **Key:** *A* = 9522, *B* = 9556, *C* = 9552, *D* = 9554, *E* = 9532

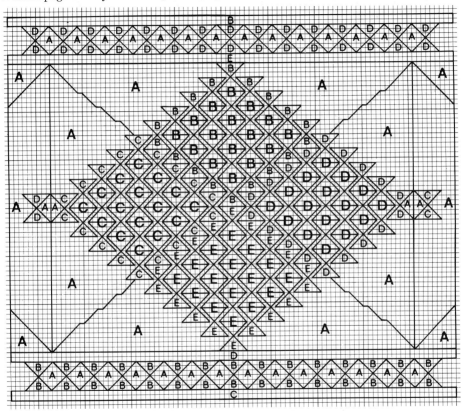

◀ **Tile Pattern** page 79 **Key:** *A, B and C* = 9252, *D, E and F* = 9254, *G* = 0842 *(Stranded Cotton), H* = 0213 *(Stranded Cotton)*

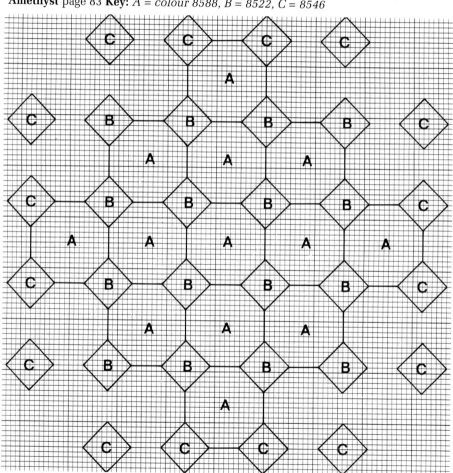

Blue Tile page 85 **Key:** *A and B = 8820, A (top) = 8804, C = 8818, D and E = 8814*

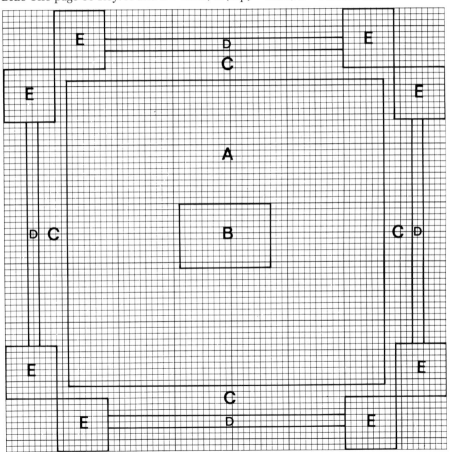

Rya page 87 **Key:** *A and H = colour 8092, B and I = 8116, C = 8120, D and K = 8140, E and L = 8064, G = 8004, and F = 9648*

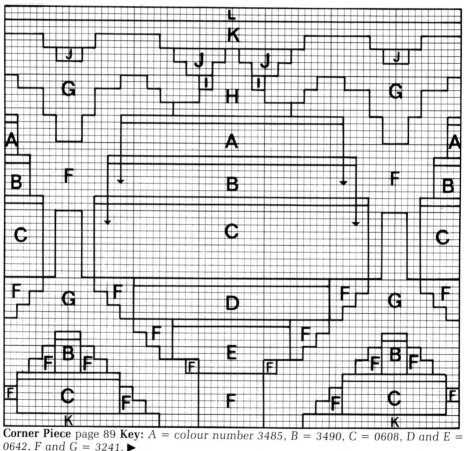

Corner Piece page 89 **Key:** *A = colour number 3485, B = 3490, C = 0608, D and E = 0642, F and G = 3241.* ▶

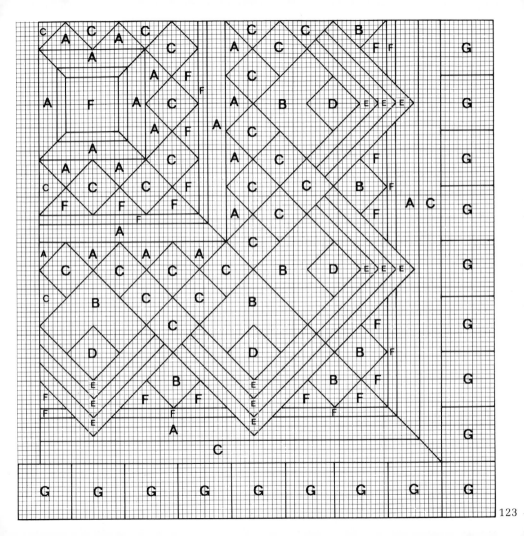

123

Stained Glass page 91 **Key:** $A = 8692$, $B = 8608$, $C = 8588$, $D = 8488$, $E = 8458$, $F = 9100$, $G = 9096$ and solid areas = 9800

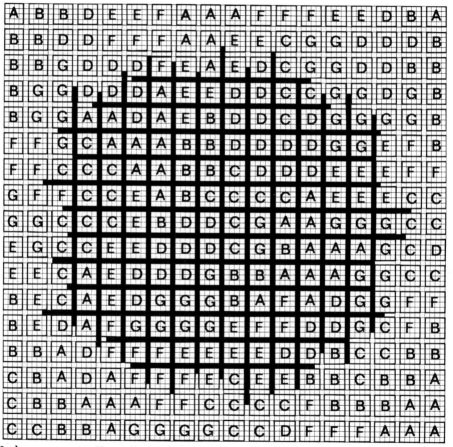

Harbour page 93 **Key:** $A = colour\ number\ 9074$, $B = 8782$, $C = 8104$, $D = 8004$, $E = 8054$, F and $G = 9368$, $H = 8628$, I and $J = 8792$, $K = 9452$ ▶

124

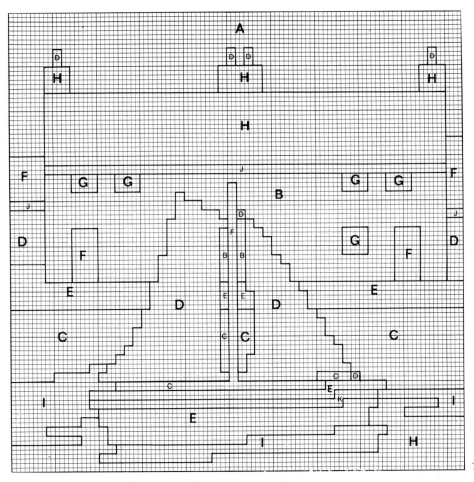

125

Trellis page 95 **Key:** *A = colour number 8522, B = 8782, C = 8004, D = 8834, E = 8806*

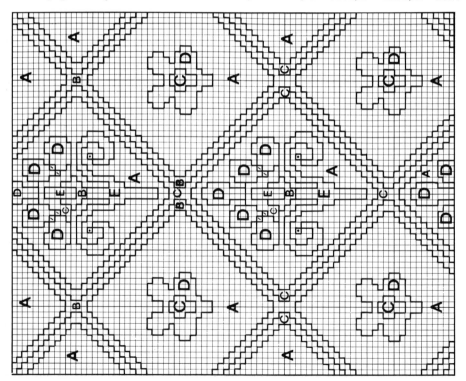

Sheep page 96 **Key:** *A and B = colour number 9052, C = 9362, D and E = 9800, F = 9162, G = 8106, H = 9396, I = 9080, J = 8968, K = 8990, L = 8922, M = 8818, N = 8772, O = 9214*

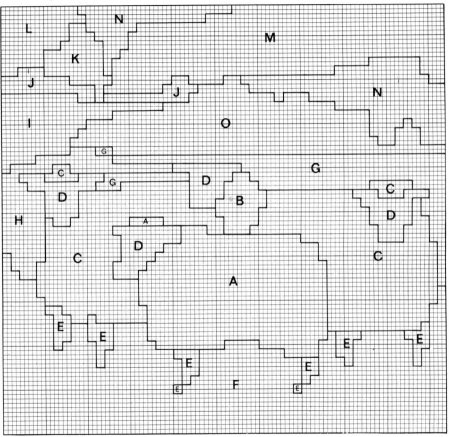

A catalogue record for this book is available from the
British Library

0 7153 0631 6

First published 1989
Reprinted 1990, 1991 (twice), 1992, 1993 (twice), 1994, 1995
This edition published 1997

Printed in Italy
by New Interlitho Italia SpA
for David & Charles
Brunel House   Newton Abbot   Devon